A LOVE GOD GREATLY JOURNAL

Contents

Welcome

WE ARE GLAD you have decided to join us in this Bible study! First of all, please know that you have been prayed for! It is not a coincidence you are participating in this study.

Our prayer for you is simple: that you will grow closer to our Lord as you dig into His Word each and every day! As you develop the discipline of being in God's Word on a daily basis, our prayer is that you will fall in love with Him even more as you spend time reading from the Bible.

Each day before you read the assigned scripture(s), pray and ask God to help you understand it. Invite Him to speak to you through His Word. Then listen. It's His job to speak to you, and it's your job to listen and obey.

Take time to read the verses over and over again. We are told in Proverbs to search and you will find: "Search for it like silver, and hunt for it like hidden treasure. Then you will understand" (Prov. 2:4–5 NCV).

We are thrilled to provide these different resources for you as you participate in our online Bible study:

- *God with Us* Study Journal

- Reading Plan

- Weekly Blog Posts (Mondays, Wednesdays, and Fridays)

- Weekly Memory Verses

- Weekly Monday Videos

- Weekly Challenges

- Online Community: Facebook, Twitter, Instagram, LoveGodGreatly.com

- Hashtags: #LoveGodGreatly

All of us here at Love God Greatly can't wait for you to get started, and we hope to see you at the finish line. Endure, persevere, press on—and don't give up! Finish well what you are beginning today. We will be here every step of the way, cheering you on! We are in this together. Fight to rise early, to push back the stress of the day, to sit alone and spend time in God's Word! Let's see what God has in store for you in this study! Journey with us as we learn to love God greatly with our lives!

Our Community

LOVE GOD GREATLY (LGG) is a beautiful community of women who use a variety of technology platforms to keep each other accountable in God's Word.

We start with a simple Bible reading plan, but it doesn't stop there.

Some women gather in homes and churches locally, while others connect online with women across the globe. Whatever the method, we lovingly lock arms and unite for this purpose: to love God greatly with our lives.

In today's fast-paced technology-driven world, it would be easy to study God's Word in an isolated environment that lacks encouragement or support, but that isn't the intention here at Love God Greatly. God created us to live in community with Him and with those around us.

We need each other, and we live life better together.

Because of this, would you consider reaching out and doing this study with someone?

All of us have women in our lives who need friendship, accountability, and have the desire to dive into God's Word on a deeper level. Rest assured we'll be studying right alongside you—learning with you, cheering for you, enjoying sweet fellowship, and smiling from ear to ear as we watch God unite women together—intentionally connecting hearts and minds for His glory.

It's pretty unreal, this opportunity we have to grow not only closer to God through this study but also to each other. So here's the challenge: call your mom, your sister, your grandma, the girl across the street, or the college friend across the country. Gather a group of girls from your church or workplace, or meet in a coffee shop with friends you have always wished you knew better. Utilize the beauty of connecting online for inspiration and accountability, and take opportunities to meet in person when you can.

Arm-in-arm and hand-in-hand, let's do this thing…together.

How to SOAP

We really want you to know that.

We're proud of you for making the commitment to be in God's Word, to be reading it each day and applying it to your life, the beautiful life our Lord has given you.

In this study we offer you a study journal to accompany the verses we are reading. This journal is designed to help you interact with God's Word and learn to dig deeper, encouraging you to slow down and reflect on what God is saying to you that day.

At Love God Greatly, we use the SOAP Bible study method. Before beginning, let's take a moment to define this method and share why we recommend using it during your quiet time.

Why SOAP It?

It's one thing to simply read Scripture. But when you interact with it, intentionally slowing down to really reflect on it, suddenly words start popping off the page. The SOAP method allows you to dig deeper into Scripture and see more than you would if you simply read the verses and then went on your merry way. Please take the time to SOAP through our Bible studies and see for yourself how much more you get from your daily reading. You'll be amazed.

What Does SOAP Mean?

S stands for **Scripture**. Physically write out the verses. You'll be amazed at what God will reveal to you just by taking the time to slow down and write out what you are reading!

O stands for **observation**. What do you see in the verses that you're reading? Who is the intended audience? Is there a repetition of words? What words stand out to you?

A stands for **application**. This is when God's Word becomes personal. What is God saying to you today? How can you apply what you just read to your own personal life? What changes do you need to make? Is there action you need to take?

P stands for **prayer**. Pray God's Word back to Him. Spend time thanking Him. If He has revealed something to you during this time in His Word, pray about it. If He has revealed some sin that is in your life, confess. And remember, He loves you dearly.

Follow This Example

Scripture: Read and write out Colossians 1:5–8.

> "The faith and love that spring from the hope stored up for you in heaven and about which you have already heard in the true message of the gospel that has come to you. In the same way, the gospel is bearing fruit and growing throughout the whole world— just as it has been doing among you since the day you heard it and truly understood God's grace. You learned it from Epaphras, our dear fellow servant, who is a faithful minister of Christ on our behalf, and who also told us of your love in the Spirit" (NIV).

Observation: Write what stands out to you.

> When you combine faith and love, you get hope. We must remember that our hope is in heaven; it is yet to come. The gospel is the Word of truth. The gospel is continually bearing fruit and growing from the first day to the last. It just takes one person to change a whole community…Epaphras.

Application: Apply this scripture to your own life.

> God used one man, Epaphras, to change a whole town. I was reminded that we are simply called to tell others about Christ; it's God's job to spread the gospel, to grow it, and have it bear fruit. I felt today's verses were almost directly spoken to Love God Greatly women: "The gospel is bearing fruit and growing throughout the whole world—just as it has been doing among you since the day you heard it and truly understood God's grace."

It's so fun when God's Word comes alive and encourages us in our current situation! My passionate desire is that all the women involved in our LGG Bible study will understand God's grace and have a thirst for His Word. I was moved by this quote from my Bible commentary today: "God's Word is not just for our information, it is for our transformation."

Prayer: Pray over this.

> Dear Lord, please help me to be an "Epaphras," to tell others about You and then leave the results in Your loving hands. Please help me to understand and apply personally what I have read today to my life, thereby becoming more and more like You each and every day. Help me to live a life that bears the fruit of faith and love, anchoring my hope in heaven, not here on earth. Help me to remember that the best is yet to come!

SOAP It Up

Remember, the most important ingredients in the SOAP method are your interaction with God's Word and your application of His Word to your life:

> Blessed is the one who does not walk in step with the wicked or stand in the way that sinners take or sit in the company of mockers, but whose delight is in the law of the LORD, and who meditates on his law day and night. That person is like a tree planted by streams of water, which yields its fruit in season and whose leaf does not wither—whatever they do prospers. (Ps. 1:1–3, NIV)

Reading Plan

Week 1 - The Promise of a Savior (as seen throughout the OT)

		Read	SOAP
Monday		Genesis 3:14-15	Genesis 3:15
Tuesday		Micah 5:2-5	Micah 5:2
Wednesday		Isaiah 9:6-7	Isaiah 9:6
Thursday		Isaiah 7:14	Isaiah 7:14
Friday		2 Samuel 7:10-13	2 Samuel 7:12-13
Response Day			

Week 2 - The Coming of Our Savior

		Read	SOAP
Monday	It meant leaving Heaven	2 Corinthians 8:9; John 6:38	John 6:38
Tuesday	It meant taking on flesh	John 1:1-5;14	John 1:14
Wednesday	It meant veiling His glory	Philippians 2:5-7	Philippians 2:5-7
Thursday	It meant being rejected by people	John 1:9-13	John 1:11
Friday	It meant being forsaken by God	Matthew 27:46	Matthew 27:46
Response Day			

Week 3 - The Reason for His Coming

		Read	SOAP
Monday	To redeem the lost	Galatians 4:4-5	Galatians 4:4-5
Tuesday	To bring good news to the afflicted	Isaiah 61:1-3	Isaiah 61:1
Wednesday	To purchase for himself a people	Titus 2:14; Revelation 5:9	Revelation 5:9
Thursday	To build a kingdom	Daniel 7:13-14	Daniel 7:14
Friday	To glorify His name	Romans 11: 33-36; Luke 2:14	Romans 11:36
Response Day			

Week 4 - The response

		Read	SOAP
Monday	Mary	Luke 1:46-56	Luke 1:46-49
Tuesday	The Shepherds	Luke 2:8-20	Luke 2:20
Wednesday	The Angels	Hebrews 1:6; Luke 2:8-14	Luke 2:13-14; Hebrews 1:6
Thursday	The Magi	Matthew 2:1-12	Matthew 2:10-11
Friday	His People	Revelation 7:9-10; 19:6-10	Revelation 7:7-10
Response Day			

Goals

WE BELIEVE it's important to write out goals for this study. Take some time now and write three goals you would like to focus on as you begin to rise each day and dig into God's Word. Make sure and refer back to these goals throughout the next eight weeks to help you stay focused. You can do it!

My goals are:

1.

2.

3.

Signature: _____

Date: _____

Introduction

COME, THOU LONG EXPECTED JESUS

HAVE YOU EVER wondered what God was doing all those years before the incarnation? Or why he chose to wait as long as he did before the incarnation became a reality? I have. But God's plan of salvation through the birth and death of Jesus was not something he thought of in a moment of boredom. It was a plan that was determined before the foundation of the world. A plan that was, and continues to be, extremely intricate.

Bit by bit God revealed the Savior, who would come to save his people from their sins. This Advent started back in Genesis and continued throughout the entire Old Testament. As the Children's Story Book Bible states, "Every story whispers his name." The time of the Old Testament was a season of preparing and waiting.

Do you know this hymn?

> Come, Thou long expected Jesus
> Born to set Thy people free;
> From our fears and sins release us,
> Let us find our rest in Thee.
> Israel's strength and consolation,
> Hope of all the earth Thou art;

This Christmas hymn beautifully expresses the longing that the Old Testament people must have felt. But now we can rejoice because the long awaited Savior has been born! This is good news of great joy because it means salvation has come and sin has been defeated.

In the Old Testament the people of God looked forward in anticipation for the coming of the Messiah. This Advent required lots of waiting, trusting, and patience.

Even now we are in a season of Advent, aren't we? We are waiting expectantly for our Savior to return. To rescue us, once and for all, from the presence of sin and fear, to make all things right and beautiful, and for us to dwell in his kingdom and walk forever by his side. The Advent we are in also requires waiting, trusting, and patience.

The hope that Israel had is the same hope that we have today as well. They had full confidence in the promises of God and in a Messiah who would come to rescue his people.

In our 2016 Advent study we will look at some of the Old Testament promises of the Savior and the humility that would characterize him. We will study why He came and the response of various people in the Christmas story, including how we should respond to Jesus as well.

"The Christmas message is that there is hope for a ruined humanity – hope of pardon, hope of peace with God, hope of glory – because at the Father's will Jesus became poor, and was born in a stable so that thirty years later He might hang on a cross."

J.I. Packer

Week 1

Week 1 Challenge (Note: You can find this listed in our Monday blog post):

Prayer focus for this week: Spend time praying for your family members.

	Praying	Praise
Monday		
Tuesday		
Wednesday		
Thursday		
Friday		

For to us a child is born, to us a son is given;
and the government shall be upon his shoulder,
and his name shall be called,
Wonderful Counselor, Mighty God,
Everlasting Father, Prince of Peace.

ISAIAH 9:6

Scripture for Week 1

MONDAY   *GENESIS 3:14-15*

¹⁴ The Lord God said to the serpent,

"Because you have done this,
    cursed are you above all livestock
    and above all beasts of the field;
on your belly you shall go,
    and dust you shall eat
    all the days of your life.
¹⁵ I will put enmity between you and the woman,
    and between your offspring and her offspring;
he shall bruise your head,
    and you shall bruise his heel."

TUESDAY   *MICAH 5:2-5*

² But you, O Bethlehem Ephrathah,
    who are too little to be among the clans of Judah,
from you shall come forth for me
    one who is to be ruler in Israel,
whose coming forth is from of old,
    from ancient days.
³ Therefore he shall give them up until the time
    when she who is in labor has given birth;
then the rest of his brothers shall return
    to the people of Israel.
⁴ And he shall stand and shepherd his flock in the strength of
the Lord,
    in the majesty of the name of the Lord his God.
And they shall dwell secure, for now he shall be great
    to the ends of the earth.
⁵ And he shall be their peace.
When the Assyrian comes into our land
    and treads in our palaces,
then we will raise against him seven shepherds
    and eight princes of men;

WEDNESDAY   *ISAIAH 9:6-7*

⁶ For to us a child is born,
   to us a son is given;
and the government shall be upon his shoulder,
   and his name shall be called
Wonderful Counselor, Mighty God,
   Everlasting Father, Prince of Peace.
⁷ Of the increase of his government and of peace
   there will be no end,
on the throne of David and over his kingdom,
   to establish it and to uphold it
with justice and with righteousness
   from this time forth and forevermore.
The zeal of the Lord of hosts will do this.

THURSDAY   *ISAIAH 7:14*

¹⁴ Therefore the Lord himself will give you a sign. Behold, the virgin shall conceive and bear a son, and shall call his name Immanuel.

FRIDAY   *2 SAMUEL 7:10-13*

¹⁰ And I will appoint a place for my people Israel and will plant them, so that they may dwell in their own place and be disturbed no more. And violent men shall afflict them no more, as formerly, ¹¹ from the time that I appointed judges over my people Israel. And I will give you rest from all your enemies. Moreover, the Lord declares to you that the Lord will make you a house. ¹² When your days are fulfilled and you lie down with your fathers, I will raise up your offspring after you, who shall come from your body, and I will establish his kingdom. ¹³ He shall build a house for my name, and I will establish the throne of his kingdom forever.

Monday

READ: Genesis 3:14-15

SOAP: Genesis 3:15

Scripture - Write out the **Scripture** passage for the day.

Observations - Write down 1 or 2 **observations** from the passage.

Monday

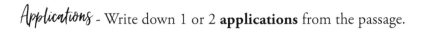

Applications - Write down 1 or 2 **applications** from the passage.

Pray - Write out a **prayer** over what you learned from today's passage.

-Visit our website today for the corresponding blog post!-

Tuesday

READ: Micah 5:2-5
SOAP: Micah 5:2

Scripture - Write out the **Scripture** passage for the day.

Observations - Write down 1 or 2 **observations** from the passage.

Tuesday

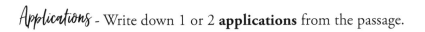

Applications - Write down 1 or 2 **applications** from the passage.

Pray - Write out a **prayer** over what you learned from today's passage.

Wednesday

READ: Isaiah 9:6-7
SOAP: Isaiah 9:6

Scripture - Write out the **Scripture** passage for the day.

Observations - Write down 1 or 2 **observations** from the passage.

Wednesday

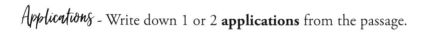

Applications - Write down 1 or 2 **applications** from the passage.

Pray - Write out a **prayer** over what you learned from today's passage.

-Visit our website today for the corresponding blog post!-

Thursday

READ: Isaiah 7:14
SOAP: Isaiah 7:14

Scripture - Write out the **Scripture** passage for the day.

Observations - Write down 1 or 2 **observations** from the passage.

Thursday

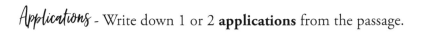

Applications - Write down 1 or 2 **applications** from the passage.

Pray - Write out a **prayer** over what you learned from today's passage.

Friday

READ: 2 Samuel 7:10-13
SOAP: 2 Samuel 7:12-13

Scripture - Write out the **Scripture** passage for the day.

Observations - Write down 1 or 2 **observations** from the passage.

Friday

Applications - Write down 1 or 2 **applications** from the passage.

Pray - Write out a **prayer** over what you learned from today's passage.

-Visit our website today for the corresponding blog post!-

Reflection Questions

1. Look up or google the word "protoevangelium." Why is Gen. 3:15 called the protoevangelium?

2. What are some of the prophecies we see in the Old Testament about the coming of Jesus?

3. In Isaiah 9:6 we are given a number of names and functions of Jesus. Each one is prefaced with an adjective (he is not just counselor, but wonderful counselor ...). List out all of the adjectives and what it tells us about Jesus.

4. What does the name Emanuel mean and how should that impact your everyday life?

5. Waiting is hard. How do you think the people in the Old Testament kept their hope alive? How do you keep your hope alive as you wait for Jesus to return?

My Response

Week 2

Week 2 Challenge (Note: You can find this listed in our Monday blog post):

Prayer focus for this week: Spend time praying for your country.

	Praying	Praise
Monday		
Tuesday		
Wednesday		
Thursday		
Friday		

And the Word became
flesh and dwelt among us,
and we have seen his glory, glory as
of the only Son from the Father,
full of grace and truth.

JOHN 1:14

Scripture for Week 2

MONDAY   *2 CORINTHIANS 8:9*

⁹ For you know the grace of our Lord Jesus Christ, that though he was rich, yet for your sake he became poor, so that you by his poverty might become rich.

JOHN 6:38

³⁸ For I have come down from heaven, not to do my own will but the will of him who sent me.

TUESDAY   *JOHN 1:1-5*

¹ In the beginning was the Word, and the Word was with God, and the Word was God. ² He was in the beginning with God. ³ All things were made through him, and without him was not any thing made that was made. ⁴ In him was life, and the life was the light of men. ⁵ The light shines in the darkness, and the darkness has not overcome it.

JOHN 1:14

¹⁴ And the Word became flesh and dwelt among us, and we have seen his glory, glory as of the only Son from the Father, full of grace and truth.

WEDNESDAY   *PHILIPPIANS 2:5-7*

⁵ Have this mind among yourselves, which is yours in Christ Jesus, ⁶ who, though he was in the form of God, did not count equality with God a thing to be grasped, ⁷ but emptied himself, by taking the form of a servant, being born in the likeness of men.

THURSDAY   *JOHN 1:9-13*

⁹ The true light, which gives light to everyone, was coming into the world. ¹⁰ He was in the world, and the world was made

through him, yet the world did not know him. [11] He came to his own, and his own people did not receive him. [12] But to all who did receive him, who believed in his name, he gave the right to become children of God, [13] who were born, not of blood nor of the will of the flesh nor of the will of man, but of God.

FRIDAY   *MATTHEW 27:46*

[46] And about the ninth hour Jesus cried out with a loud voice, saying, "Eli, Eli, lema sabachthani?" that is, "My God, my God, why have you forsaken me?"

Monday

READ: 2 Corinthians 8:9; John 6:38

SOAP: John 6:38

Scripture - Write out the **Scripture** passage for the day.

Observations - Write down 1 or 2 **observations** from the passage.

Monday

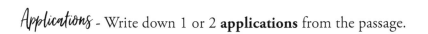

Applications - Write down 1 or 2 **applications** from the passage.

Pray - Write out a **prayer** over what you learned from today's passage.

-Visit our website today for the corresponding blog post!-

Tuesday

READ: John 1:1-5;14
SOAP: John 1:14

Scripture - Write out the **Scripture** passage for the day.

Observations - Write down 1 or 2 **observations** from the passage.

Tuesday

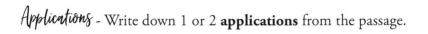

Applications - Write down 1 or 2 **applications** from the passage.

Pray - Write out a **prayer** over what you learned from today's passage.

Wednesday

READ: Philippians 2:5-7
SOAP: Philippians 2:5-7

Scripture - Write out the **Scripture** passage for the day.

Observations - Write down 1 or 2 **observations** from the passage.

Wednesday

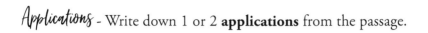

Applications - Write down 1 or 2 **applications** from the passage.

Pray - Write out a **prayer** over what you learned from today's passage.

-Visit our website today for the corresponding blog post!-

Thursday

READ: John 1:9-13
SOAP: John 1:11

Scripture - Write out the **Scripture** passage for the day.

Observations - Write down 1 or 2 **observations** from the passage.

Thursday

Applications - Write down 1 or 2 **applications** from the passage.

Pray - Write out a **prayer** over what you learned from today's passage.

Friday

READ: Matthew 27:46
SOAP: Matthew 27:46

Scripture - Write out the **Scripture** passage for the day.

Observations - Write down 1 or 2 **observations** from the passage.

Friday

Applications - Write down 1 or 2 **applications** from the passage.

Pray - Write out a **prayer** over what you learned from today's passage.

-Visit our website today for the corresponding blog post!-

Reflection Questions

1. Beside's leaving heaven, what else did Jesus "leave behind" in order to dwell on earth? (Read 2 Cor. 8:9 for help.)

2. Did Jesus appear human or actually become human? Why is this important?

3. Jesus was fully man and fully God, so what does it mean that he emptied himself?

4. Jesus came to save the lost but he is rejected by many. Read John 3:19-21 for more insight. In what ways do we as believers reject Jesus?

5. On the cross Jesus experienced being forsaken by the Father. What do you think this means? How is this good news for us?

My Response

Week 3

Week 3 Challenge (Note: You can find this listed in our Monday blog post):

Prayer focus for this week: Spend time praying for your friends.

	Praying	Praise
Monday		
Tuesday		
Wednesday		
Thursday		
Friday		

But when the fullness of time
had come, God sent forth his Son,
born of woman, born under the law,
to redeem those who were under the law,
so that we might receive
adoption as sons.

GALATIANS 4:45

Scripture for Week 3

MONDAY

⁴ But when the fullness of time had come, God sent forth his Son, born of woman, born under the law, ⁵ to redeem those who were under the law, so that we might receive adoption as sons.

TUESDAY

ISAIAH 61:1-3

¹ The Spirit of the Lord God is upon me,
   because the Lord has anointed me
to bring good news to the poor;
   he has sent me to bind up the brokenhearted,
to proclaim liberty to the captives,
   and the opening of the prison to those who are bound;

² to proclaim the year of the Lord's favor,
   and the day of vengeance of our God;
   to comfort all who mourn;

³ to grant to those who mourn in Zion—
   to give them a beautiful headdress instead of ashes,
the oil of gladness instead of mourning,
   the garment of praise instead of a faint spirit;
that they may be called oaks of righteousness,
   the planting of the Lord, that he may be glorified.

WEDNESDAY

TITUS 2:14

¹⁴ who gave himself for us to redeem us from all lawlessness and to purify for himself a people for his own possession who are zealous for good works.

REVELATION 5:9

⁹ And they sang a new song, saying,

"Worthy are you to take the scroll
   and to open its seals,

for you were slain, and by your blood you ransomed people for God

from every tribe and language and people and nation,

THURSDAY *DANIEL 7:13-14*

[13] "I saw in the night visions,
and behold, with the clouds of heaven
there came one like a son of man,
and he came to the Ancient of Days
and was presented before him.

[14] And to him was given dominion
and glory and a kingdom,
that all peoples, nations, and languages
should serve him;
his dominion is an everlasting dominion,
which shall not pass away,
and his kingdom one
that shall not be destroyed.

FRIDAY *ROMANS 11: 33-36*

[33] Oh, the depth of the riches and wisdom and knowledge of God! How unsearchable are his judgments and how inscrutable his ways!

[34] "For who has known the mind of the Lord,
or who has been his counselor?"

[35] "Or who has given a gift to him
that he might be repaid?"

[36] For from him and through him and to him are all things. To him be glory forever. Amen.

LUKE 2:14

[14] "Glory to God in the highest,
and on earth peace among those with whom he is pleased!"

Monday

READ: Galatians 4:4-5
SOAP: Galatians 4:4-5

Scripture - Write out the **Scripture** passage for the day.

Observations - Write down 1 or 2 **observations** from the passage.

Monday

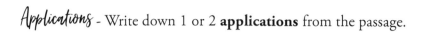

Applications - Write down 1 or 2 **applications** from the passage.

Pray - Write out a **prayer** over what you learned from today's passage.

-Visit our website today for the corresponding blog post!-

Tuesday

READ: Isaiah 61:1-3
SOAP: Isaiah 61:1

Scripture - Write out the **Scripture** passage for the day.

Observations - Write down 1 or 2 **observations** from the passage.

Tuesday

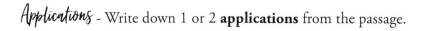

Applications - Write down 1 or 2 **applications** from the passage.

Pray - Write out a **prayer** over what you learned from today's passage.

Wednesday

READ: Titus 2:14; Revelation 5:9
SOAP: Revelation 5:9

Scripture - Write out the **Scripture** passage for the day.

Observations - Write down 1 or 2 **observations** from the passage.

Wednesday

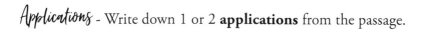

Applications - Write down 1 or 2 **applications** from the passage.

Pray - Write out a **prayer** over what you learned from today's passage.

-Visit our website today for the corresponding blog post!-

Thursday

READ: Daniel 7:13-14
SOAP: Daniel 7:14

Scripture - Write out the **Scripture** passage for the day.

Observations - Write down 1 or 2 **observations** from the passage.

Thursday

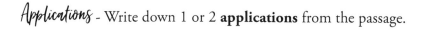

Applications - Write down 1 or 2 **applications** from the passage.

Pray - Write out a **prayer** over what you learned from today's passage.

Friday

READ: Romans 11: 33-36; Luke 2:14
SOAP: Romans 11:36

Scripture - Write out the **Scripture** passage for the day.

Observations - Write down 1 or 2 **observations** from the passage.

Friday

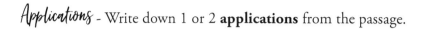

Applications - Write down 1 or 2 **applications** from the passage.

Pray - Write out a **prayer** over what you learned from today's passage.

-Visit our website today for the corresponding blog post!-

Reflection Questions

1. List all the reasons why Jesus came to earth.

2. How is the news of Christ's birth "good news to the poor"? How does it "bind up the brokenhearted," "proclaim liberty to the captives," and open "the prison to those who are bound"? Which one of these can you identify with the most?

3. Jesus came to build for himself a kingdom. What will this kingdom be like? What parts are you looking forward to the most?

4. Why does Jesus save people? (Look at 1 Peter 2:9 for help.)

5. How does the birth of Jesus glorify God?

My Response

Week 4

Week 4 Challenge (Note: You can find this listed in our Monday blog post):

Prayer focus for this week: Spend time praying for your church.

	Praying	Praise
Monday		
Tuesday		
Wednesday		
Thursday		
Friday		

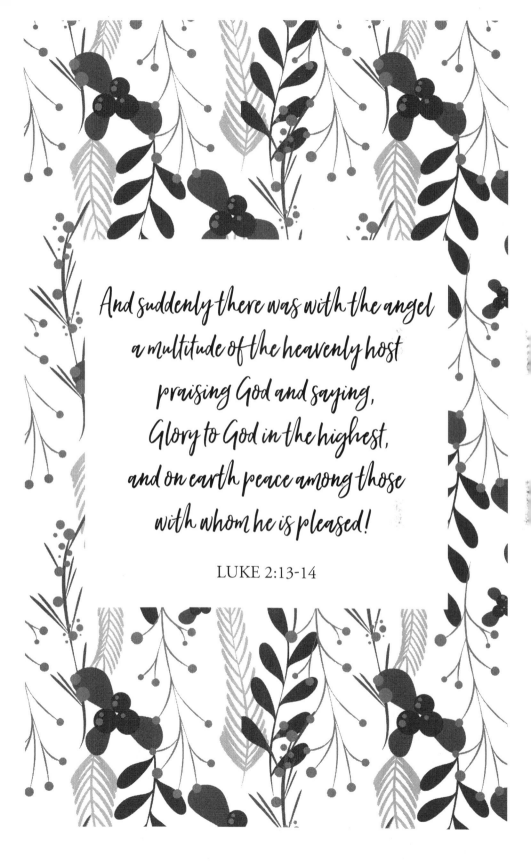

And suddenly there was with the angel a multitude of the heavenly host praising God and saying, Glory to God in the highest, and on earth peace among those with whom he is pleased!

LUKE 2:13-14

Scripture for Week 4

MONDAY

LUKE 1:46-56

⁴⁶ And Mary said,

"My soul magnifies the Lord,
⁴⁷   and my spirit rejoices in God my Savior,
⁴⁸ for he has looked on the humble estate of his servant.
    For behold, from now on all generations will call me blessed;
⁴⁹ for he who is mighty has done great things for me,
    and holy is his name.
⁵⁰ And his mercy is for those who fear him
    from generation to generation.
⁵¹ He has shown strength with his arm;
    he has scattered the proud in the thoughts of their hearts;
⁵² he has brought down the mighty from their thrones
    and exalted those of humble estate;
⁵³ he has filled the hungry with good things,
    and the rich he has sent away empty.
⁵⁴ He has helped his servant Israel,
    in remembrance of his mercy,
⁵⁵ as he spoke to our fathers,
    to Abraham and to his offspring forever."

⁵⁶ And Mary remained with her about three months and returned to her home.

TUESDAY

LUKE 2:8-20

⁸ And in the same region there were shepherds out in the field, keeping watch over their flock by night. ⁹ And an angel of the Lord appeared to them, and the glory of the Lord shone around them, and they were filled with great fear. ¹⁰ And the angel said to them, "Fear not, for behold, I bring you good news of great joy that will be for all the people. ¹¹ For unto you is born this day in the city of David a Savior, who is Christ the Lord. ¹² And this will be a sign for you: you will find a baby wrapped in swaddling cloths and lying in a manger." ¹³ And suddenly there was with the

angela multitude of the heavenly host praising God and saying,

¹⁴ "Glory to God in the highest,
and on earth peace among those with whom he is pleased!"

¹⁵ When the angels went away from them into heaven, the shepherds said to one another, "Let us go over to Bethlehem and see this thing that has happened, which the Lord has made known to us." ¹⁶ And they went with haste and found Mary and Joseph, and the baby lying in a manger. ¹⁷ And when they saw it, they made known the saying that had been told them concerning this child. ¹⁸ And all who heard it wondered at what the shepherds told them. ¹⁹ But Mary treasured up all these things, pondering them in her heart. ²⁰ And the shepherds returned,glorifying and praising God for all they had heard and seen, as it had been told them.

WEDNESDAY   *HEBREWS 1:6*

⁶ And again, when he brings the firstborn into the world, he says,
"Let all God's angels worship him."

LUKE 2:8-14

⁸ And in the same region there were shepherds out in the field, keeping watch over their flock by night. ⁹ And an angel of the Lord appeared to them, and the glory of the Lord shone around them, and they were filled with great fear. ¹⁰ And the angel said to them, "Fear not, for behold, I bring you good news of great joy that will be for all the people. ¹¹ For unto you is born this day in the city of David a Savior, who is Christ the Lord. ¹² And this will be a sign for you: you will find a baby wrapped in swaddling cloths and lying in a manger." ¹³ And suddenly there was with the angela multitude of the heavenly host praising God and saying,

¹⁴ "Glory to God in the highest,
and on earth peace among those with whom he is pleased!"

THURSDAY   *MATTHEW 2:1-12*

¹Now after Jesus was born in Bethlehem of Judea in the days of Herod the king, behold, wise men from the east came to Jerusalem, ² saying, "Where is he who has been born king of the Jews? For we saw his star when it rose and have come to worship him." ³ When Herod the king heard this, he was troubled, and all Jerusalem with him; ⁴ and assembling all the chief priests and scribes of the people, he inquired of them where the Christ was to be born. ⁵ They told him, "In Bethlehem of Judea, for so it is written by the prophet:

⁶ "'And you, O Bethlehem, in the land of Judah,
   are by no means least among the rulers of Judah;
for from you shall come a ruler
   who will shepherd my people Israel.'"

⁷ Then Herod summoned the wise men secretly and ascertained from them what time the star had appeared. ⁸ And he sent them to Bethlehem, saying, "Go and search diligently for the child, and when you have found him, bring me word, that I too may come and worship him." ⁹ After listening to the king, they went on their way. And behold, the star that they had seen when it rose went before them until it came to rest over the place where the child was. ¹⁰ When they saw the star, they rejoiced exceedingly with great joy. ¹¹ And going into the house, they saw the child with Mary his mother, and they fell down and worshiped him. Then, opening their treasures, they offered him gifts, gold and frankincense and myrrh. ¹² And being warned in a dream not to return to Herod, they departed to their own country by another way.

FRIDAY   *REVELATION 7:9-10*

⁹ After this I looked, and behold, a great multitude that no one could number, from every nation, from all tribes and peoples and languages, standing before the throne and before the Lamb, clothed in white robes, with palm branches in their hands, ¹⁰ and crying out with a loud voice, "Salvation belongs to our God who sits on the throne, and to the Lamb!"

[6] Then I heard what seemed to be the voice of a great multitude, like the roar of many waters and like the sound of mighty peals of thunder, crying out,

"Hallelujah!
For the Lord our God
    the Almighty reigns.
[7] Let us rejoice and exult
    and give him the glory,
for the marriage of the Lamb has come,
    and his Bride has made herself ready;
[8] it was granted her to clothe herself
    with fine linen, bright and pure"—
for the fine linen is the righteous deeds of the saints.

[9] And the angel said to me, "Write this: Blessed are those who are invited to the marriage supper of the Lamb." And he said to me, "These are the true words of God." [10] Then I fell down at his feet to worship him, but he said to me, "You must not do that! I am a fellow servant with you and your brothers who hold to the testimony of Jesus. Worship God." For the testimony of Jesus is the spirit of prophecy.

Monday

READ: Luke 1:46-56
SOAP: Luke 1:46-49

Scripture - Write out the **Scripture** passage for the day.

Observations - Write down 1 or 2 **observations** from the passage.

Monday

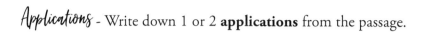

Applications - Write down 1 or 2 **applications** from the passage.

Pray - Write out a **prayer** over what you learned from today's passage.

-Visit our website today for the corresponding blog post!-

Tuesday

READ: Luke 2:8-20
SOAP: Luke 2:20

Scripture - Write out the **Scripture** passage for the day.

Observations - Write down 1 or 2 **observations** from the passage.

Tuesday

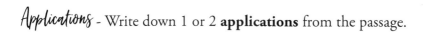

Applications - Write down 1 or 2 **applications** from the passage.

Pray - Write out a **prayer** over what you learned from today's passage.

Wednesday

READ: Hebrews 1:6; Luke 2:8-14
SOAP: Luke 2:13-14; Hebrews 1:6

Scripture - Write out the **Scripture** passage for the day.

Observations - Write down 1 or 2 **observations** from the passage.

Wednesday

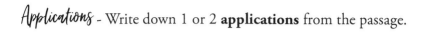

Applications - Write down 1 or 2 **applications** from the passage.

Pray - Write out a **prayer** over what you learned from today's passage.

-Visit our website today for the corresponding blog post!-

Thursday

READ: Matthew 2:1-12
SOAP: Matthew 2:10-11

Scripture - Write out the **Scripture** passage for the day.

Observations - Write down 1 or 2 **observations** from the passage.

Thursday

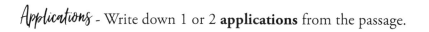

Applications - Write down 1 or 2 **applications** from the passage.

Pray - Write out a **prayer** over what you learned from today's passage.

Friday

READ: Revelation 7:9-10; 19:6-10
SOAP: Revelation 7:7-10

Scripture - Write out the **Scripture** passage for the day.

Observations - Write down 1 or 2 **observations** from the passage.

Friday

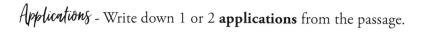

Applications - Write down 1 or 2 **applications** from the passage.

Pray - Write out a **prayer** over what you learned from today's passage.

-Visit our website today for the corresponding blog post!-

Reflection Questions

1. What does it mean to "magnify" something? In what ways can we magnify the Lord in our lives?

2. The Shepherds are praising God for all that they had seen and heard? What were those things. What do you see and hear in your life that you can praise God for?

3. The angels sing about peace on earth and are praising God for it. But if we look at the world peace seems to be missing. What peace are they talking about?

4. The Magi bring with them gifts of gold, frankincense and myrrh. What is the significance of each one? https://www.crossway.org/blog/2010/12/whyweregoldincenseandmyrrhappropriategiftsforjesus/ http://www.gotquestions.org/goldfrankincensemyrrh.html

5. It is easy to get caught up in all the holiday fun. What are one or two things that we can do to help keep our eyes on Jesus?

My Response

How Can You Know That You Are Forgiven?

Know these truths from God's Word...

God loves you.

Even when you're feeling unworthy and like the world is stacked against you, God loves you - *yes, you* - and He has created you for great purpose.

> God's Word says, "God so loved the world that He gave His one and only Son, Jesus, that whoever believes in Him shall not perish, but have eternal life" (John 3:16).

Our sin separates us from God.

We are all sinners by nature and by choice, and because of this we are separated from God, who is holy.

> God's Word says, "All have sinned and fall short of the glory of God" (Romans 3:23).

Jesus died so that you might have life.

The consequence of sin is death, but your story doesn't have to end there! God's free gift of salvation is available to us because Jesus took the penalty for our sin when He died on the cross.

God's Word says, "For the wages of sin is death, but the free gift of God is eternal life in Christ Jesus our Lord" (Romans 6:23); "God demonstrates His own love toward us, in that while we were yet sinners, Christ died for us" (Romans 5:8).

Jesus lives!

Death could not hold Him, and three days after His body was placed in the tomb Jesus rose again, defeating sin and death forever! He lives today in heaven and is preparing a place in eternity for all who believe in Him.

God's Word says, "In my Father's house are many rooms. If it were not so, would I have told you that I go to prepare a place for you? And if I go and prepare a place for you, I will come again and will take you to myself, that where I am you may be also" (John 14:2-3).

Yes, you can KNOW that you are forgiven.

Accept Jesus as the only way to salvation...

Accepting Jesus as your Savior is not about what you can do, but rather about having faith in what Jesus has already done. It takes recognizing that you are a sinner, believing that Jesus died for your sins, and asking for forgiveness by placing your full trust in Jesus's work on the cross on your behalf.

God's Word says, "If you confess with your mouth that Jesus is Lord and believe in your heart that God raised him from the dead, you will be saved. For with the heart one believes and is justified, and with the mouth one confesses and is saved" (Romans 10:9-10).

Practically, what does that look like? With a sincere heart, you can pray a simple prayer like this:

God,

I know that I am a sinner.

I don't want to live another day without embracing

the love and forgiveness that You have for me.

I ask for Your forgiveness.

I believe that You died for my sins and rose from the dead.

I surrender all that I am and ask You to be Lord of my life.

Help me to turn from my sin and follow You.

Teach me what it means to walk in freedom as I live under Your grace,

and help me to grow in Your ways as I seek to know You more.

Amen.

If you just prayed this prayer (or something similar in your own words), would you email us at info@lovegodgreatly.com? We'd love to help get you started on this exciting journey as a child of God!

Welcome, friend. We're so glad you're here...

LOVE GOD GREATLY exists to inspire, encourage, and equip women all over the world to make God's Word a priority in their lives.

-INSPIRE-

women to make God's Word a priority in their daily lives through our Bible study resources.

-ENCOURAGE-

women in their daily walks with God through online community and personal accountability.

-EQUIP-

women to grow in their faith, so that they can effectively reach others for Christ.

Love God Greatly consists of a beautiful community of women who use a variety of technology platforms to keep each other accountable in God's Word.

We start with a simple Bible reading plan, but it doesn't stop there.

Some gather in homes and churches locally, while others connect online with women across the globe. Whatever the method, we lovingly lock arms and unite for this purpose...

to Love God Greatly with our lives.

At *Love God Greatly*, you'll find real, authentic women. Women who are imperfect, yet forgiven. Women who desire less of us, and a whole lot more of Jesus. Women who long to know God through his Word, because we know that Truth transforms and sets us free. ***Women who are better together, saturated in God's Word and in community with one another.***

Love God Greatly is a 501 (C) (3) non-profit organization. Funding for Love God Greatly comes through donations and proceeds from our online Bible study journals and books. LGG is committed to providing quality Bible study materials and believes finances should never get in the way of a woman being able to participate in one of our studies. All LGG journals and translated journals are available to download for free from LoveGodGreatly.com for those who cannot afford to purchase them. Our journals and books are also available for sale on Amazon. Search for "Love God Greatly" to see all of our Bible study journals and books. 100% of proceeds go directly back into supporting Love God Greatly and helping us inspire, encourage and equip women all over the world with God's Word.

THANK YOU for partnering with us!

What we offer:

18 + Translations | Bible Reading Plans | Online Bible Study
Love God Greatly App | 80 + Countries Served
Bible Study Journals & Books | Community Groups

Each Love God Greatly study includes:

Three Devotional Corresponding Blog Posts | Monday Vlog Videos
Memory Verses | Weekly Challenge | Weekly Reading Plan
Reflection Questions And More!

Other Love God Greatly studies include:

David | Ecclesiastes | Growing Through Prayer | Names Of God
Galatians | Psalm 119 | 1st & 2nd Peter | Made For Community | Esther
The Road To Christmas | The Source Of Gratitude | You Are Loved

Made in the USA
Lexington, KY
30 November 2016